The Wild Prairie

The Wild Prairie

A Natural History
of the
Western Plains

by Tim Fitzharris

Oxford University Press
Toronto 1983

In Memory of Art Fitzharris

Acknowledgments

I am grateful to a number of people who freely assisted me in making this book. Jim Fitzharris accompanied me on many field trips, preparing the meals, transporting equipment, setting up photographic blinds and cheerfully carrying out numerous other unsavory chores. David Tomlinson provided invaluable and enthusiastic assistance in finding and leading me to bird nests suitable for photography. In a variety of ways, Don Li-Leger provided skilled help in a number of photographic undertakings. John Doremus, Mark Hilliard and Vicki Marks at the Bureau of Land Management in Boise, Idaho gave needed advice and assistance in photographing ·birds of prey along the Snake River. Bayne Stanley made special arrangements for me to use photographic equipment supplied by **Canon** . Most important, my thanks go to Sheryl Fitzharris for help in editing the pictures, critical reading of the text and typing of the manuscript. Her unfailing support and enthusiasm for a project that extended over a number of years added much to my enjoyment of the work.

Produced by Roger Boulton
Designed by Fortunato Aglialoro (Studio 2 Graphics)

Canadian Cataloguing in Publication Data

Fitzharris, Tim, 1948–
The wild prairie

ISBN 0-19-540438-6

1. Natural history—Prairie Provinces.* 2. Natural history—Great Plains.   I. Title.

QH106.P7F47   508.712   C83-098239-6

© Oxford University Press (Canadian Branch) 1983
Oxford is a trademark of Oxford University Press

ISBN 0-19-540438-6

1 2 3 4 - 6 5 4 3

Printed in Hong Kong by
Everbest Printing Company Limited

Contents

Introduction

A VAST EXPANSE of wild grassland once covered most of the interior region of North America. It stretched from what is now Edmonton, Alberta, south almost to Mexico City, a distance of more than 4000 km/2500 mi. The steep walls of the Rocky Mountains marked its western boundary. Along its eastern edge the grasslands were hemmed in by the northern spruce forests of Canada and the central hardwood forests of the United States.

This tract of land was a mixture of many natural communities, all of which shared a single characteristic: grass dominated the vegetative pattern. More than 60 different grass species grew here. As a group they were adaptable to a variety of conditions—scorching heat or petrifying cold, floods or extended periods of drought. Highly nutritious, they provided a complete diet for many animals. Not only were the grasses hardy and high in food value but with favourable weather they became amazingly productive. In years of adequate rainfall the Prairies supported wildlife in unsurpassed abundance.

There were tall-grass prairies, mixed-grass prairies, short-grass prairies, bunch-grass prairies, mesquite prairies, and parklands which were mixtures of grasses and trees. The boundaries of these various types shifted continually owing to fires, changes in rainfall, grazing by large herbivores and other factors. The southern prairies were dry and hot and had many shrubs; the northern regions were more cool and humid. Over this open, far-flung landscape the wind blew almost constantly.

Driving through the Prairies today it is difficult to imagine what life there was like before the arrival of the white man. By conservative estimates this ocean of grass supported 45,000,000 of the continent's largest beast, the American bison; and a beast it was—a bull stood 2 m/6 ft to the top of its great humped shoulders and weighed as much as a dozen full-grown men. The prairies also were swarming with one of the swiftest animals on earth, the pronghorn antelope. Most authorities believe they rivalled the bison in number. In addition, there were other large-hoofed mammals—mule deer, white-tailed deer, and elk—that roamed the plains in numbers unheard of today.

These immense herds were shadowed by a host of carnivores—giant plains grizzlies, scavenging foxes, and packs of lanky prairie wolves and wiry coyotes. Ready to pounce from the thickets were lynx, bobcats and cougars.

Nevertheless, the huge populations of large mammals were still far exceeded by the numbers of smaller creatures. Hordes of jackrabbits, cottontails, mice, shrews, voles, ground-squirrels, gophers, weasels, badgers, skunks, and raccoons scurried among the grasses, churned up the sod and burrowed into the rich soil. There were astronomical numbers of prairie dogs; thousands of their colonies, or towns, were scattered over the prairies. One in Texas spread for more than 65,000 sq. km/25,000 sq. mi. and contained more than 400,000,000 prairie dogs.

The bird life was no less rich. Bobolinks, pipits, meadowlarks, horned larks, and many species of sparrows serenaded the plains from the grasstops. Sage grouse, sharp-tailed grouse and prairie chickens strutted on traditional dancing grounds during the breeding season. Hovering, wheeling and diving about them were hawks, eagles, falcons, and vultures. The marshes and potholes were astir with pelicans, cranes, herons, sandpipers, swans, geese, and ducks. During the fall and spring the skies were filled with streams of migrating birds of every description.

Today only a fraction of this life remains. The most productive prairies, the tall-grass and mixed-grass regions, have given way to agriculture. The native vegetation has been ploughed under and destroyed. In its place grow straight rows of corn, symmetrical swaths of wheat, barley and rye—cereal crops to feed the peoples of the world. All the buffalo have disappeared except for a few small herds kept in game reserves. The once ubiquitous prairie dogs can be found only in a handful of isolated towns. A mere hundred thousand or so pronghorns remain, most of them in dry, sparsely populated regions. Roads, highways, train tracks, canals, ditches, fences, power lines, and cultivated windbreaks have chopped the landscape into millions of pieces. Undoubtedly the prairies have lost much of their former grandeur. But in many areas the big skies and rolling countryside still have the magic of unspoiled wilderness.

Most of the pictures in this book were taken in Alberta, Saskatchewan, Montana and North Dakota, in parts of the prairies called the High Plains, where some areas remain relatively undisturbed by man. Pronghorns and mule deer still roam unfenced tracts of short grass prairie that is too dry for growing crops or grazing livestock. There are thousands of potholes and sloughs that have yet to be drained to provide extra acres of tillable land. River valleys, coulees and ravines too steep to be farmed, or too meagerly wooded to be logged, retain a good part of their wild heritage.

If we could look at these High Plains in cross-section, we would see that their reputation for flatness is no exaggeration. The plains are, however, tilted, rising steadily from east to west at a rate of about 2 m per km/10 ft per mi. until they reach the Rocky Mountain foothills. Their eastern edge is not so clearly defined, but it is marked by a low east-facing escarpment, a belt of hills, ridges and

eroded terrain, that extends from southern Saskatchewan to Texas and roughly bisects the states of North Dakota, South Dakota, Nebraska, Kansas, and Oklahoma. The escarpment marks a broad transition zone between the tall-grass prairie of the east (now the corn belt) and the short-grass prairies of the High Plains.

A mantle of eroded materials that were carried down from the mountains by streams and rivers forms the top layer of the plains. Once the rushing, debris-laden waters reached the foot of the mountains they slowed, spread out, and deposited their rich sediments in a wide arc. As older streams dried up and new watercourses developed in different areas the debris was deposited in overlapping layers. Over thousands of years a single, gently sloping plain was laid down. The eastern escarpment marks the furthest extent of this process.

In the ages that followed, the rivers went through continuing cycles of cutting, eroding and depositing so that the original topography became modified. Glaciers came in from the north, scraping and gouging the land, laying down sediments, creating lakes and water channels before receding. The wind left its mark as well, building soils and sculpting stretches of sand dunes. Today a traveller on the High Plains not only encounters the sweep of level prairies but also sees elevated plateaus, the weird formations of the badlands, rocky canyons, coulees, mesas, lakes, potholes, and river bottomlands. This variety of landforms affords niches for many different plants and animals.

The lushness of the grass of the High Plains is determined by rainfall. Humid winds sweeping in from the Pacific begin to lose their moisture on encountering the coastal mountain ranges. By the time this air rolls down the eastern slope of the Rockies and onto the plains, it has been wrung dry. The average yearly rainfall of the plains is not more than 51 cm/20 in. and western regions receive far less. In this arid environment grasses seldom exceed knee-height. During the spring, rain and melting snow soak the soil, the grass flourishes and the terrain takes on a pale-green hue. The air is cool, clear and perfumed by the burgeoning vegetation. By summertime the increase in temperature and incessant winds have dried out the plains and the landscape is tawny brown. Dust clouds the atmosphere whenever it is kicked up by any slight disturbance.

Of the many wild grasses found on the High Plains, blue grama is the most common. Short, tough and growing in thick tufts, it provides excellent nutrition for grazing animals, especially during the fall and winter when other grasses lose their food value. Its sickle-shaped flower spikes make it easy to identify. On the eastern margin of the plains, rainfall is heaviest. Here, the grass is taller and thicker, and species such as needle grass and little blue stem gain prominence.

Grass, of course, is not the only type of vegetation on the plains. A significant portion of the ground-cover consists of broad-leaved herbs (forbs), many of which produce flowers of great beauty. Blooming from early spring until fall, these wildflowers enliven the prairies with a riot of colours and intriguing designs. Purple crocus, broomweed, scarlet mallow, moss phlox, pasture sage, prickly pear cactus, sunflowers, golden rods, and asters are some of the more common varieties.

Shrubs also contribute to the richness of the flora. Some are found in patches on the open prairie, but aspen groves, slough margins, bottomlands, stream banks, and coulees provide the best growing conditions. The numerous species of wild roses and sage brush are perhaps the best known shrubs. Other species are also prevalent: buckbrush, chokecherry, snowberry, and red-osier dogwood are widespread; in arid regions salt bush, yucca and rabbit brush are found.

Although the High Plains grasslands once teemed with animals, the spread of agriculture greatly decreased the significance of the region as wildlife habitat. Two other aspects of the prairie environment have been less affected: the wetlands (lakes, marshes, sloughs, potholes) and the riverlands (coulees, ravines, river valleys). These habitats are the last refuge for many kinds of wildlife. Unfortunately their abundance is being eroded steadily by urban encroachment and more exploitative farming practices.

In years of average precipitation there are more than 8,000,000 sloughs and potholes on the Canadian prairies alone. Run-off from the surrounding land carries soil particles into these depressions, enriching the water and the bottom sediments. The vegetation that results has proved of little direct benefit to man, but it is vital to wildlife.

Cattails and bulrushes are the characteristic emergent plants found along the shoreline, but reed grass, sedges and water horsetail are also common. As the water deepens, floating plants, such as waterlily and the pea-sized duck weed, become prevalent. Growing below the surface are various species of algae, watermilfoil and pondweeds. Despite the apparent lushness of these larger plants, the greatest food producer is phyto-plankton—the microscopic drifting forms of algae.

This plant community supports a complex web of animal life. The smallest creatures to feed on this vegetative matter are the zoo plankton. Each slough harbours billions of these tiny organisms. They are consumed by slightly larger animals such as sponges, hydras, snails, and fairy shrimp. This unseen galaxy of life that seeths, twists, twitches, wiggles and crawls below the surface ultimately becomes food for the dragonflies, turtles, frogs, muskrats, shorebirds, pelicans, and waterfowl. For-

tunately this system of complex, intertwining food chains is highly efficient and the wetlands nurture remarkable numbers of higher animals, especially birds. Seventy per cent of the entire North American duck population, for example, is bred in the sloughs and potholes of the prairies.

With the grasslands almost completely given over to agriculture or other forms of development, the riverlands, like the potholes and sloughs, have become a focus of wildlife activity. The forested river valleys are the most obvious examples of this type of habitat, but coulees, creek beds, ravines, and wooded hillsides (usually north-facing) also fall into this category. These areas generally are low lying and snow readily accumulates in them. Also, these depressions are shielded from the drying effects of the sun and wind. The extra moisture that results allows large woody plants to grow.

Except in very dry regions, most riverbanks on the High Plains are covered to some degree with trees and shrubs. The make-up of these plant communities is varied and depends on such factors as soil type, precipitation, sunlight and grazing by animals. Willows, birches and cottonwoods of various species, and box-elder are widespread. Frequently forming pure stands, the trembling aspen and balsam poplar are common on the northern

part of the plains. Being less tolerant of growing conditions, other trees—ash, maple, cherry, juniper, spruce, and pine—are more localized in distribution.

Trees are the dominant plants in these riverland habitats and the protection they provide permits the formation of a varied understory of shrubs and herbs. Within these communities live many animals totally adapted for life in a forest environment—tree squirrels, porcupines, beavers, lynx, blackbears, woodpeckers, nuthatches, and chickadees, for example. However, riverlands also provide shelter and reproductive sites for many species that feed on the grasslands, such as the prairie falcon, red-tailed hawk, mule deer, and coyote.

This brief review of the natural history of the western plains will give readers who are not familiar with the region some background to the pictures that follow. The photographs were taken over a five year period. During this time I spent hundreds of hours hidden in blinds, photographing the intimate day-to-day activities of the wildlife. I tried to record aspects of this habitat which few people have the opportunity to see and enjoy for themselves. I hope this book will contribute to a wider appreciation and concern for the natural treasures of our western grasslands.

Grasslands

With wide eyes and perked ears, a coyote scans the surrounding grasslands.

FOLLOWING PAGES: A small herd of pronghorn antelope on the autumn prairie.

The pronghorn buck gathers a harem of up to 15 does during the mating season.

THE PRONGHORN ANTELOPE is one of North America's smallest hoofed mammals. It stands not much taller than a large dog (91 cm/3 ft at the shoulder) and weighs about 45 kgm/100 lbs. A pronghorn's eyes, however, are larger than a horse's. On the open treeless plains, it can spot the movement of its chief predators (men and coyotes) up to 6 km/ 3.7 mi. in the distance. Members of a herd pass warning signals by raising the patch of long white hairs which encircle the rump. The fleetest land animal on the continent, the pronghorn has a smooth level gait that carries it over the prairie at speeds of 70 km/43.5 mi. per hour with occasional bursts estimated to exceed 80 km/50 mi. per hour. From a population that once rivalled that of the bison, the number of pronghorns dwindled to only 20,000 in the early part of the century due to ruthless hunting. Today the herds have recovered and their survival as a wild species is not in jeopardy.

The flowers of the pin cushion cactus develop into soft, sweet berries that are eaten by pronghorns.

The black-necked stilt frequents flooded fields and pastures of the West.

HIGHLY SPECIALIZED PLANTS—grasses of nearly 200 species—form the climax vegetation pattern of the prairies. Few plants are as hardy or as well adapted to survival. Grass can be trampled by countless hooves, chewed off to the ground, frozen, drowned, dessicated, or burnt by wind-driven fire, and yet survive to thrive anew once better conditions return. Self-pollinating, grass needs only a breath of wind to start the process of seed production. Once developed, these tough seeds are equipped with kite-like appendages which transport them on the wind; or they may have hooks that snag on a passing fox or bison. The roots are perhaps most amazing of all. Sending branches out horizontally, they are able to send up new grass stems. In times of drought the microscopic root hairs can probe the soil to take in the most infinitesimal bits of moisture. The roots of some species grow to depths of 3 m/9.8 ft., and the total system, including the root hairs and many small branches, can be over 500 km/311 mi. long.

In the spring, a rolling short-grass prairie is dotted with puddles of meltwater.

THE COTTONTAIL is an inhabitant of fencerows, meadows and shrubby areas. During the day it rests quietly in an overgrown hollow or brushpile, grooming and digesting its food. The cottontail's eliminated pellets are of two types: brown faecal pellets and soft green ones composed of only partially digested plant matter. The latter are sorted out, chewed and re-ingested by the rabbit much in the way a cow chews its cud. Once the sun sets, the cottontail ventures out to feed on young grasses and herbs such as goldenrod, buttercup, wild strawberry, and smartweed. During the winter the diet changes to bark, twigs and buds of young trees and shrubs.

Like other small prairie herbivores, the cottontail is ecologically important, converting plant growth into meat that is vital to the carnivores. Many predators feed on the relatively defenseless cottontail—foxes, coyotes, weasels, great-horned owls, and hawks. Nevertheless, it thrives, primarily due to its compatibility to cultivated lands and remarkable reproductive capacity.

A cottontail feeds on tender grasses during the summer.

For many prairie animals, grass constitutes a complete and healthy diet.

SOARING HIGH on thermal air currents, the rasping scream of the red-tailed hawk is a familiar sound over the plains. Wherever rodents are plentiful, there are likely to be a number of these large (wingspan 1.5 m./5 ft) and powerful birds. Readily distinguished by its chestnut-red tail feathers, the hunting red-tail usually perches atop a tree or telephone pole overlooking a ground-squirrel or prairie-dog colony, or a field rich in mice. Like other raptors, it has powerful binocular vision eight times keener than a human's.

From its hunting perch, a red-tailed hawk inspects the field below for an unwary mouse or ground-squirrel.

When prey is spotted, the hawk launches itself, thrusting forward with a few powerful wingbeats and then gliding swiftly and silently in for the kill, striking the careless rodent with its piercing talons.

The red-tail builds a bulky nest of sticks and twigs in an aspen grove or in a stand of cottonwoods along a river. The incubation period for the two or three eggs lasts around one month. About six weeks after being hatched, the young are on the wing, joining their parents in patrol over the grasslands.

Feeding largely on waste grains, the ring-necked pheasant is a frequent prey of large hawks.

At its cliffside nest, a ferruginous hawk prepares to dismember a ground-squirrel for its hungry young.

OF THE MANY SPECIES of prairie ground-squirrels, the Richardson's ground-squirrel is one of the most widespread and common. It lives in loose colonies on the open plains, preferring sandy soils that afford easy burrowing. The underground workings are a maze of narrow passageways and interconnected chambers which may extend to 15 m./49 ft. There are usually more than half-a-dozen mounded exits which serve as observation posts. Here the little squirrel often rests, sitting upright, paws on its chest, as it watches over the surrounding plains.

Like most ground-squirrels, the Richardson's is active during daylight hours, making short excursions to feed on grasses and other soft-stemmed plants. Away from the burrow it is vulnerable to attack by all the large soaring hawks as well as by the swift prairie falcon. If danger is imminent, the ground-squirrel gallops for safety and, issuing a barrage of shrill chattering notes, plunges into its hole.

FOLLOWING PAGES: A coyote pauses for a serenade on the open prairie.

A Richardson's ground-squirrel chirps in alarm at the entrance to its burrow.

The thick, woolly hide of the bison helps it survive the prairie's harsh winters.

THE AMERICAN BISON is the largest mammal on the continent. A bull weighs up to 900 kgm (2000 lbs) and its massive, humped shoulders stand taller than the average man. Before Europeans arrived on the plains, an estimated 45 million buffalo roamed the lush grasslands. With its heavy head slung low for easy grazing and a thick, shaggy coat to protect it from the worst blizzards, the bison completely dominated the ecology. The vast, wandering herds were followed by a host of predators—giant plains grizzlies, prairie wolves, coyotes, and scavenging foxes. By the late 1800s there remained only twenty wild bison over the immense sweep of the central grasslands. The familiar story of their demise is at once colourful and tragic. Today a few thousand bison are found roaming freely in a number of western parks.

TO MANY PEOPLE the coyote symbolizes the wide open spaces of the West. A slim, buff-coloured creature resembling a small collie, the 'prairie songdog' is best known for its night-time serenades. On still evenings, its calls—a quick series of yelps ending off in a falsetto howl—drift into the sleepy streets of small prairie towns. Often the shrill yips are issued up by a pack as it assembles on a hilltop in preparation for a hunting excursion.

The agile coyote will feed on almost anything it can catch and kill, but nearly ninety per cent of its diet has been found to consist of rabbits, hares, mice, ground-squirrels, and carrion. Small domestic animals such as lambs, calves and poultry are occasionally taken. Despite the coyotes' beneficial control of rodents, thousands have been exterminated—supposedly for the good of agriculture. Recently their economic and aesthetic value has been recognized and the species is protected in some areas.

In the grasslands of the West, coyotes course the fields in search of mice and voles.

White-tailed bucks bound across a meadow.

SECLUDED IN THE TREES and brush of a coulee or aspen grove, white-tailed deer rest and chew the cud during the day. They become active at dawn and dusk, usually foraging singly but sometimes in bands of two or three. They are primarily browsers, feeding on the twigs and buds of shrubs and saplings. Their diet is supplemented by tender grasses, forbs and fruit.

The white-tailed deer's most impressive feature is its big, flaglike tail that is almost a foot long. Brown above and snow-white below, the deer flicks it from side to side or hoists it high when in flight, flashing the snowy white under-surface. The billowy tail is in striking contrast to the deer's trim outline, rich, reddish-fawn coat, and white belly, throat and eye ring. The bucks are particularly attractive, having graceful antlers formed by a pair of main, forward-sweeping beams, with a number of smaller tines branching upward.

FOLLOWING PAGES: In a snowy meadow, a mule deer pauses alertly.

Storm clouds gather on the prairie horizon.

A variety of grasses, forbs and shrubs make a rich habitat for wildlife.

GROWING IN ASSOCIATION with the prairie grasses are many other types of plants—weeds, wildflowers, cacti and shrubs. They are found practically everywhere—in patches on the prairie, in coulees, along fencerows, roadsides and riverbanks. Adding tremendously to the richness and diversity of the prairie ecology, this vegetation is utilized as food and shelter by most wildlife of the region. The flowering parts produce nectar for bees, wasps, butterflies, moths and other insects. Relished by many birds and rodents are the berries, seeds, hips and other fruits of such plants as the wild rose, western snowberry, ground-plum and Saskatoon berry. The pronghorn, bison, mule deer and white-tailed deer browse on the leaves, stems and twigs. Many wild prairie plants arrived with the early settlers as stray seeds in a sack of grain. Generally thought of as weeds, some—like sweet clover, dandelion, sow thistle, or wild mustard—are nevertheless beautiful and of value to wildlife.

Chewing a grass stem, a mule deer directs its ears at a strange sound.

THE MULE DEER is one of the most commonly seen large mammals of the prairies. It is readily distinguished from the white-tailed deer by its smaller, black-tipped tail. For an hour or two after daybreak and once again after the sun has set, small groups venture out of thickets to graze on the grasses and forbs of the open prairie. During the winter the roaming herds increase in size, sometimes associating with pronghorns as they feed on twigs of sagebrush, buckbrush and other shrubs. At this time the bands are a mix of varied ages and sexes and are led by experienced does, the bucks having become quite docile once their antlers are shed. When alarmed by predators—feral dogs, coyotes, men, lynx, cougars, or bobcats—they take flight, bouncing gracefully across the plains in a distinctive stiff-legged gait.

To reach the nectar of blue camas, an insect must crash through the pollen coated stamens.

THROUGHOUT THE LATE SPRING and summer the splendid gold and purple blooms of wild gaillardia form vivid clumps of colour on the tawny prairie landscape. Growing best on dry plains and hillsides, the gaillardia grows to 61 cm/24 in. high, has an abundance of greyish, hairy leaves, and flower heads about 8 cm/3 in. in diameter. Once the yellow rays fall, the central disc develops into a dry, hairy ball of scaly seeds.

Rising to about knee height, the blue camas produces an elongated cluster of flowers, each with six delicate petals. During June and July wet meadows and bottomlands are carpeted with the mauve-blue blooms. For centuries an essential food source for the plains Indians, the thick onion-like bulbs were dug up with sticks and baked in ground ovens to be eaten at once or stored as a winter food supply.

Wild gaillardia grows among prairie grasses.

SPECIALIZED FOR FEEDING on the pollen and honey of wildflowers, bees form a large group of insects encompassing more than 3500 species in North America. Many types have elongated mouthparts which enable them to probe deeply into the blooms. Instrumental in the pollination process of many flowering plants, bees pick up pollen in the short, stiff hairs that cover their bodies and transport it to other flowers. In many species the female's hind legs have a special pollen-collecting apparatus. The bee combs pollen from the body hairs into the basket, which appears as a large yellow bundle when full. Honeybees and bumblebees are the only types that live in colonies and produce and store honey. The multitude of other species are solitary, the female constructing her own nesting tunnel underground.

A bumblebee alights on the prickly flowerhead of a bull thistle.

The flowers of marsh ragwort provide pollen and nectar for honey bees.

THE LOW LARKSPUR grows in rich black soils of sheltered coulees and low hills of the grasslands. The flashy electric-blue bloom actually consists of five sepals (modified leaves) surrounding four smaller petals. The two upper petals are lighter in colour and combine with the uppermost sepal to form the long characteristic spur. All larkspurs are poisonous to cattle, which are unfortunately attracted by the flavour of the leaves.

Like so many plants of low rainfall areas, the scarlet mallow is densely covered with soft white hairs that lend a greyish cast to the leaves and stem. A true prairie wildflower, the mallow prefers light sandy soils. Its woody stems grow in spreading, mat-like bunches. The numerous flowers—only 1 – 1½ cm/½ – ¾ in. wide—are a flaming orange-red. Growing in densely packed leafy spikes, they set the countryside aflame with colour during the late spring and early summer.

The uniquely shaped low larkspur attains a height of 20 – 50 cm/8 – 20 in.

A bee rests momentarily on the globe-shaped bloom of scarlet mallow.

By late spring the rich colour of the prairie crocus fades to ashy grey.

A ladybug beetle crawls out of a dandelion bloom.

ONE OF THE MOST renowned of western wildflowers is the ankle-high prairie crocus. Before the snow has completely disappeared from the plains, the pale purple blooms cover ridges, hillsides and high meadows, signalling the return of spring and the imminent revival of the expanse of dead, matted grasses. By early summer the purple sepals fall away and are replaced by a cluster of long, silver, feathery fruits. From these wind-dispersed plumy seeds is derived the plant's other common name, 'anemone' from the Greek *anemos*, meaning wind.

A giant wildflower with heavy nodding heads, the prairie sunflower may rise higher than a man and be up to 10 cm/4 in across. It is an annual that grows in the light sandy soil of open habitats. Developing through the summer, each brownish-yellow central floral disc becomes densely packed with seeds, familiar in form but smaller than those of cultivated sunflowers. These seeds provide food for birds and rodents during the fall and winter.

A clump of prairie sunflowers is visited by bees and other insects.

Easily identified by four eye spots on the hind wing, the painted lady butterfly lays its eggs on thistles and sunflowers.

SKIPPERS ARE STOCKY butterflies with large heads whose name is derived from their quick bouncing manner of flying. Two characteristics easily distinguish members of this family from the many hundreds of other moth and butterfly species that are to be found kiting about the grasslands: the skipper's antennae end in swollen hooks, and when at rest the forewings are held almost vertically like a butterfly's, while the rear pair lie horizontally like those of a moth.

Like most moths and butterflies, the skipper is equipped with a long coiled drinking tube (or pro-boscis), which can be unrolled deep into the flower. Nectar and juices of fallen fruit are the major food sources. Skipper caterpillars grow quickly, and most types feed almost exclusively on grasses and sedges. When fully developed the caterpillar sheathes itself in a cocoon of leaves and silk. During this life stage, its tissue breaks down into a thick liquid from which the wings, legs and body of the butterfly are miraculously formed. On emergence the adult skipper pumps fluid into its crumpled wings and sails off over the prairie.

A skipper's long proboscis probes in a thistle for nectar.

46 GRASSHOPPERS ARE TYPICAL prairie insects. In the spring the small nymphs hatch from eggs buried in the soil, squirm to the surface and shed their skins to reveal a diminutive grasshopper. Feeding on grasses and herbs, the growing young undergo five molts before reaching the mature form. As adults they are well adapted to grassland life. Their outer shell is coated with wax to prevent loss of body fluid in their dry environment. They have two pairs of wings, powerful back legs, and large, watchful, compound eyes—all of which help them to avoid capture by enemies.

Despite these physical attributes, grasshoppers are relatively easy prey for other animals. Rodents dig up their eggs. Birds eat them during every stage of development. But cold weather causes the greatest loss of life. It not only kills the nymphs in the spring but also limits egg-laying in the fall. These misfortunes may be quickly redressed during a warm summer when 10,000 eggs are to be found in as little as 0.1 sq. m/1 sq. ft of prairie. Such reproductive ability periodically produces giant locust swarms which can devastate the vegetation over extensive areas.

A short-horned grasshopper clings to a stem.

Basking on a camas bud, a long-jawed spider keeps an eye or two on its nearby web.

A badger exhibits its burly physique and uniquely patterned face.

THE BADGER IS a giant digging weasel whose chunky low-slung frame is ideally camouflaged for its grassland habitat. A large male (weighing up to 11 kgm/24 lbs) is a prodigious excavator, having stout forelimbs and long heavy claws. During the day badgers are fairly quiet, resting and sunning themselves near their big mounded burrow entrances. Once night falls they waddle out across the plains to hunt, feeding primarily on large rodents such as ground-squirrels, prairie dogs and kangaroo rats. These the badger simply digs out of the ground one after another, in time tearing up an impressive stretch of prairie. It also consumes smaller fare—mice, voles, insects, snails and birds' eggs.

The badger's mating season occurs at the end of the summer, but implantation and subsequent development of the embryo is delayed until winter. Three or four young are born in the spring and they romp and exercise about the burrow entrance while the mother is off hunting. Even after they are weaned they continue to receive food until almost full-grown.

FOLLOWING PAGES: One of the prairie's many sparrow species, the Lapland longspur is an Arctic breeder that spends the winter on the grasslands.

Patches of prairie land left uncultivated are of great benefit to wildlife.

A burrowing owl stands behind the mounded entrance to its burrow.

THE BURROWING OWL lives in open country—grasslands, sagebrush flats and deserts—particularly where rodent burrows are numerous. A small, spotted, tawny ground owl, it has long spindly legs and a short tail. In appropriate habitat its high mournful calls are often heard once the sun has set. It begins feeding at twilight, hovering frequently as it scours the ground below for a mouse, young ground-squirrel, cricket or beetle. Dragonflies, moths and bats are snatched from the air in flight.

The nest is usually situated in an abandoned ground-squirrel burrow, the owl scratching out minor adaptations with its talons. Seven to nine eggs are laid and, once old enough, the young line up on the entrance mound during the day. Their distress call is a convincing imitation of the rattling of a prairie rattlesnake.

THE WHITE-TAILED jack rabbit is one of the plains' most exciting wildlife species. All day it lies low in its form—a shallow, hidden depression—with eyes half closed and huge ears laid over its back. If flushed it leaps away, bouncing across the prairie, its slim springy legs dangling limply between each great leap. Soon its gait changes to low ground-eating strides that may cover up to 5 m/16 ft when the hare is moving at high speed. Despite their good camouflage, impressive fleetness and fair size (up to 5.4 kgm/12 lbs), jack rabbits are persistently hunted by many predators—coyotes and foxes on the ground and eagles, the soaring hawks, and great-horned owls from the air.

On the short-grass prairie, a white-tailed jack rabbit keeps a low, inconspicuous profile.

A cock sage grouse displays its unusual plumage on the springtime dancing grounds.

THE SAGE GROUSE resides permanently on sage-brush plains of central North America. By far the largest grouse on the continent (males: length 76 cm/ 30 in., weight to 3.2 kgm/7 lbs), its grey-brown plumage is patterned to match the arid environment. The soft leaves and shoots of sagebrush are the prime food source and this plant is also used for winter shelter as well as to conceal the ground nest. Owing to livestock grazing and agriculture, the range and numbers of sage grouse have been much reduced.

Most spectacular of this bird's activities is the nuptial behaviour of the males during the spring. They gather in groups of 20 to 100 or more on traditional dancing grounds—nondescript patches of prairie that have been used by many grouse generations. Here the cocks strut, inflating and shaking the drooping air sacs of their breasts, and spreading their pointed tail feathers in an arc. These displays usually begin before dawn and continue for the first several hours of daylight until, one by one, the group melts back into the sagebrush.

Dried out Russian thistles, popularly known as 'tumble-weeds', have been carried by the wind to collect in a dry creek bed.

Wetlands

In a stand of bulrushes the plumage and posture of the American bittern serve as effective camouflage.

FOLLOWING PAGES: Winging over a marsh, a great blue heron is silhouetted against the prairie sunset.

A compact school of seven mallard ducklings swims under their mother's vigilant gaze.

OF THE MANY DUCKS that thrive on the prairies, the mallard is one of the most abundant. The glossy green head and white collar make the male easy to identify, but the hen, in her mottled brown plumage, is not so easy to distinguish from other female duck species. A dark cap and dark stripe through the eye are good field marks, yet probably most distinctive is her typically duck-like call—a series of descending 'quacks'. Mallards nest in grassy meadows near sloughs or marshes. Once hatched, the ducklings are led immediately to the safety of the water.

Here they feed on seeds from sedges, bulrushes, wild rice, pond weeds and widgeon grass as well as on aquatic insects and snails.

Each year hunters fire close to 6,000 tons of lead shot at the mallard, killing nearly 5,000,000 of them. Most of the pellets miss their mark, settling to the bottom of the marsh among the seeds on which ducks feed. Once ingested the shot causes lead poisoning, bringing a slow and painful death to many more thousands of ducks each year.

A mallard hen loafs among the broken cattails of early spring.

FEEDING MOST FREQUENTLY at dawn and dusk, the black-crowned night heron stands motionless on the shore of a marsh or lake, waiting for its prey to draw near. Depending on what is available, this heron eats small fish, toads, crayfish, dragonflies, and even garter snakes. With a chunky crow-sized body and a wingspan of nearly 1.2 m/47 in., it has a readily distinguishable silhouette that is often seen against the night sky.

A young black-crowned night heron crouches in its nest, secluded among bulrushes.

On the Prairies, black-crowned night herons nest colonially in isolated, extensive stands of cattails or bulrushes. The gangly quill-covered nestlings, three or four in number, are fed regurgitated food by the adults. When six weeks old the young have developed a mottled brown plumage and are ready to fly. They pursue the adults, begging for food until they eventually learn to forage on their own.

A black-crowned night heron hunts the mudflats of a slough.

An American coot broods its feeble nestling.

ALTHOUGH ACTUALLY a member of the rail family, the American coot has many duck-like characteristics. It swims well: on the surface it moves along distinctively, pumping its head back and forth; underwater its lobed toes propel it to depths of 9 m/23 ft to gather seeds, roots, aquatic insects, and snails. Beating its wings furiously, the coot must spatter across the surface for some distance before it manages to become airborne. It flies heavily with its knobby legs trailing.

Any shallow body of water with a bit of protective vegetation will be used as nesting habitat. During courtship, coots fill the marsh with a loud assortment of cackles, whistles, croaks, grunts, and considerable splashing. Soon after hatching the fiery-coloured chicks follow the parents about the slough to be fed, for the first week returning frequently to the nest where they are brooded.

About a week after hatching, a coot chick has lost much of its orange natal down.

A female marsh hawk carries a meadow vole to her young.

ON THE PRAIRIES the buoyant, tilting flight of the marsh hawk is seen more than that of any other bird of prey. Slender, long tailed, long legged birds with wingspans exceeding 1m/3.3 ft, marsh hawks generally weigh less than a loaf of bread. They hunt wet meadows and slough margins, alternately gliding and flapping over the grasstops until a mouse, vole or small bird is spotted. Then the hawk drops quickly onto the prey, dispatching it with needle-sharp talons.

In the spring the exciting graceful courtship-flights take place, the male and female tumbling, rolling and diving after one another—necessary preliminaries to mating. The nest is built on the ground among tall grasses, bulrushes or cattails, and five eggs are usually laid. After hatching, the brood soon develops a tremendous appetite, consuming more than a dozen small rodents a day.

FOLLOWING PAGES: A lesser scaup and her downy young.

Lunchtime at a marsh hawk nest.

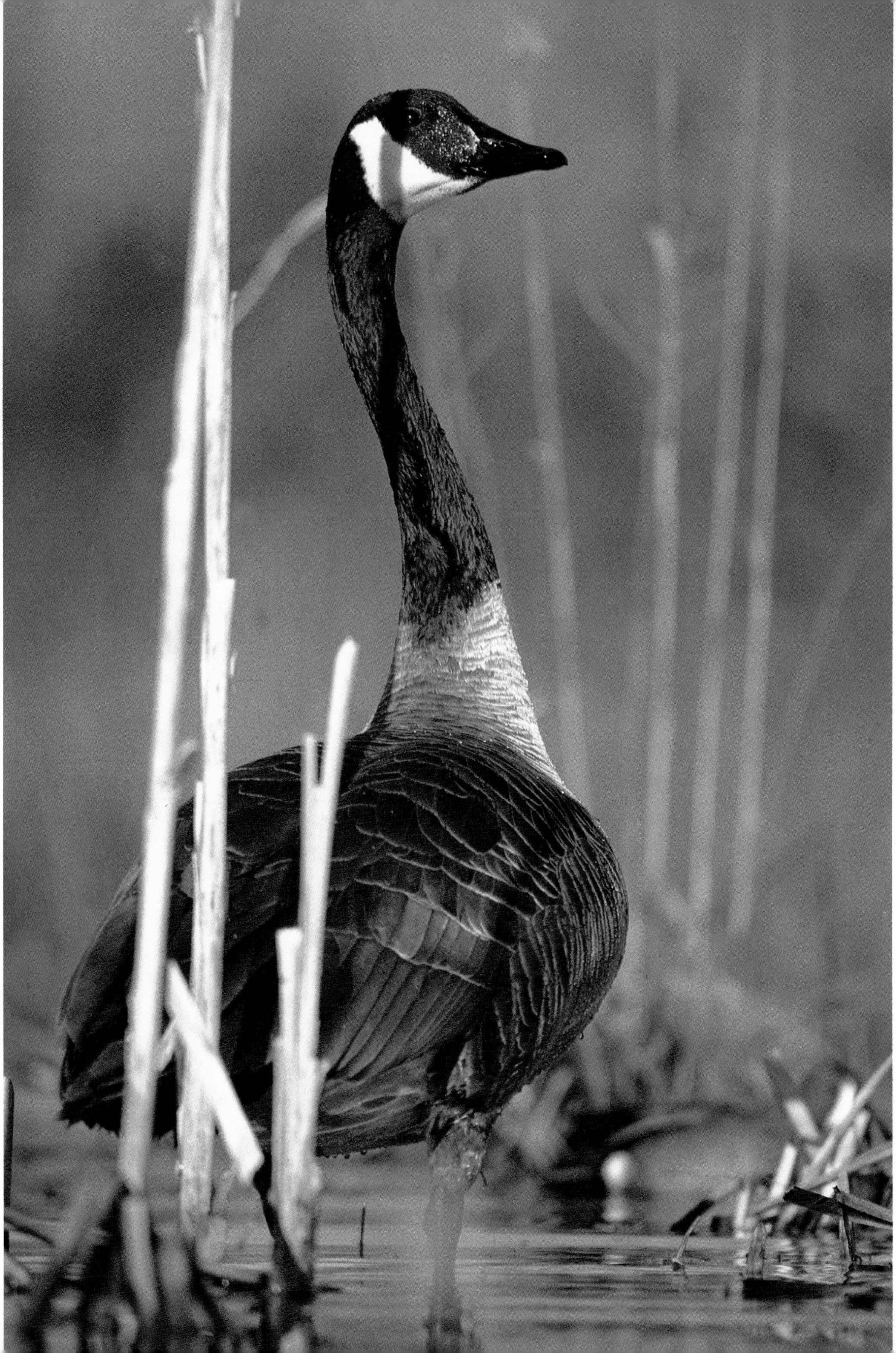

One of the millions of small sloughs that dot the prairies.

IN MARCH the musical honking of Canada geese migrating high overhead signals at last the return of spring to the prairies. Occasionally one of the straggling V formations veers towards a half-frozen lake or pothole. Breaking up into small groups, the geese glide in for a landing, planing smoothly across the water on stout, outstretched webs. Here they rest and fatten up for a few days. Essentially grazers, they crop marsh grass, pond weeds and other vegetation, using their sturdy bills. Their numbers swollen by first-year birds, the flocks reappear in the fall on their southward journey, again filling the cold, clear skies with their far-flung, melancholy songs.

On the Prairies there are a number of subspecies of Canada geese. Varying primarily in size, they range from the cackling Canada goose, weighing only 1.8 kgm/4 lbs, to the giant Canada goose, which frequently tips the scales at over 9 kgm/20 lbs. Regardless of size or voice, all Canada geese are easily identified by their black head-stockings and white cheek-patches.

Wary of intruders, a Canada goose stretches its neck in alarm.

A leopard frog floats among scattered duckweed.

OF THE VARIOUS AMPHIBIANS and reptiles that frequent the wetlands, the leopard frog is one of the most common and attractive. Strikingly patterned in green, brown and soft yellow, it has powerful legs and a smooth streamlined shape. Although hardly melodious, the distinctive, snoring chorus of these frogs drifts pleasantly over the prairie on still spring nights. Leopard frogs are voracious nocturnal predators and feed on insects, spiders and small crustaceans. The front of the tongue is attached to the lower jaw and the rearward portion is flung outward to snag anything edible that moves within range. They live along the wetland edges, entering the water frequently to chase prey, to avoid a predator or to mate. During the spring breeding season the smaller male scrambles onto the female's back, clasping her with swollen forearms and thumbs. Thus stimulated the female lays as many as 20,000 eggs, which are subsequently fertilized by secretions from the male and then soon develop into tadpoles.

As dusk settles on the marsh, many animals become more active.

THROUGHOUT THE COLD PRAIRIE WINTER painted turtles lie buried in the mud at the bottom of a pond or small lake. As the ice begins to break up they emerge, spending much of their time on sunny days basking on logs. In the late spring the female scrapes out a depression (usually near a stump close to water), deposits her eggs, covers them over and meanders back to the marsh with never a backward glance. Skunks, raccoons and snakes are always on the alert for such a rich cache and many eggs are eaten. In about three months the baby turtles hatch out. As big around as a quarter, they usually remain in the nest throughout the coming winter. Young turtles are primarily carnivorous, eating insects, tadpoles and small fish, but as they mature the diet changes primarily to plant matter. In about four years they reach 10 cm/4 in. in length and reach breeding age.

An Arctic breeder, the long-billed dowitcher passes through the prairies on spring and fall migrations.

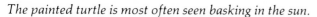

The painted turtle is most often seen basking in the sun.

A black tern prepares to set off in search of another meal for the downy nestlings.

BLACK TERNS NEST IN COLONIES on the prairies, preferring shallow grassy sloughs. Although only the size of a robin, they are aggressive toward intruders. Becoming alerted to the presence of an intruder in seconds, an angry mob of terns will take to the air, screaming abuse, and dive, one bird after another, frequently raking the victim with their tiny talons. A few minutes of this harassment is enough to discourage weasel, coyote, skunk or man from further trespass. The pandemonium subsides as the offender moves away, and the terns resettle to incubate or tend the young. By the end of August the 'kip-kip' calls of black terns are no longer heard over the prairies, most birds having moved south toward their coastal wintering grounds.

A MEMBER OF THE 'DABBLING DUCK' FAMILY, the pintail feeds by tipping up in shallow water, paddling to maintain balance and stretching its neck for seeds or succulent new growth on the bottom. In April, before farming operations commence, the hen constructs a concealed nest in a meadow or brushy area near a slough or pond. Unfortunately many nests are subsequently destroyed when stubble is burned or a pasture cultivated. Nevertheless, along with the mallard, the pintail is the most abundant western duck. It is estimated that each fall well over a million birds pass through the central prairie region alone.

Bill tucked into its feathers, a pintail rests quietly on a shallow slough.

A muskrat sits in the concealment of broken cattails.

THE MOST COMMON MAMMAL of the prairie wetlands, the muskrat is well adapted to its aquatic life style. It has webbed feet, a rudder-like tail and an air-trapping pelt that keeps it dry and warm. Its fleshy lips are able to seal the mouth behind the incisors, allowing this rodent to gnaw at vegetation without taking in water. In late summer muskrats begin lodge construction, six or seven animals working co-operatively to complete a single structure. Pond-weeds, bulrushes and cattails are gathered and plastered together to form the familiar dome-shaped structure. Once covered with snow, the lodge becomes a snug winter retreat. Muskrats remain active throughout the cold weather, leaving by an under-water passageway to feed below the ice on pond-weeds, bladderwort, milfoil and other vegetation.

The small (length 17 cm/6.5 in.), seldom-seen sora rail is a common bird of prairie marshes.

IN APRIL SMALL FLOCKS of sandhill cranes appear over the prairies. Buoyed by thermal air currents, the great birds (wingspan 2 m./6.6 ft) spiral slowly northward at high altitudes. At day's end they alight in a marsh or stubble field to feed and rest. Courtship may also be carried out, the lanky cranes springing upward on outstretched wings while their powerful gurgling songs reverberate over the flat land. Some birds remain on the prairies to nest, while others continue on to the marshes and muskegs of the tundra. Once on the breeding grounds the crane takes about three months to incubate the eggs and nourish the young to flying size. In September long skeins of cranes appear again over the ripening grainfields, now bound for their wintering grounds in California and Central America.

FOLLOWING PAGES: Sandhill cranes gather in a shallow slough.

A swarm of midges envelops a sow thistle.

INSECT LIFE ABOUNDS in the rich waters of the prairie potholes and sloughs. On warm nights in the summer and fall the water's surface is alive with endlessly whirling, darting aggregations of many types. Springtails, alder flies, stoneflies, mayflies, dragonflies and damselflies, caddisflies, water bugs and scorpions, beetles, and true flies—including midges, gnats and mosquitoes—are all likely to be represented in even the smallest pothole. However, what appears above the surface is only part of the picture. The sub-adult stages of aquatic insects— eggs, larvae and pupae—teem below the surface, feeding on each other as well as on plants and small animals. In turn they are eaten by fish, amphibians, reptiles, birds and mammals, thus becoming a vital link in the food-chain of a marsh or slough.

At dusk a variety of insects clouds the surface of a marsh.

Measuring 75 mm/3 in., the green darner is one of the largest dragonflies.

DRAGONFLIES CATCH AND EAT tremendous numbers of other insects. They have intriguing predatory characteristics—enormous, bulging, compound eyes and a freely rotating head—that give them a wide field of vision. Their legs hang basket-like beneath the strong, cutting mouthparts, ready to entrap a flying midge or mosquito and hold it while the meal progresses. The four powerful, net-veined wings work independently, enabling the insect to hover, or to fly forward and backward with great speed.

Once mating takes place the fertilized eggs are laid by the female in or near the water, hatching into naiads (larvae) a few days later. These live underwater, capturing insects, tadpoles and even small fish. Their chief weapon is a stiff, bristle-tipped, elongated lower lip that is kept folded under the head. Should prey venture near, the lip is slung outward with lighting speed, snagging the victim and pulling it into the mouth.

A white tail skimmer rests momentarily from its aerial patrolling of the shoreline.

The bronzed cutworm moth is found in the sedges and grasses that border the sloughs.

Bluet damselflies mate.

LIKE THEIR RELATIVES the dragonflies, damselflies are brightly coloured aerial predators. These two insects can be readily distinguished by the wing structure. Dragonflies extend the wings horizontally to the sides, while damselflies hold them vertically toward the rear. Damselflies are smaller than dragonflies and their large eyes bulge out to the side, while the dragonfly's eyes nearly cover the entire head.

Both types of insects mate in flight. The male (usually the more brightly coloured) first curls the tip of its abdomen forward to deposit a packet of sperm in a special chamber near its thorax. Then using special clamps, it grasps the female by the neck, thus giving her the opportunity to pick up the sperm with the tip of her own abdomen and achieving a transfer of the genetic materials.

Soon the rumpled masses of tiny male flowers of these cattails will fall away, leaving the smooth lower cylinders of female flowers, which will darken and swell into the familiar cattail shape.

FOLLOWING PAGES: Magnificent birds, with wingspans reaching 2.7 m/9 ft, white pelicans are gradually disappearing from the prairies.

A pair of redheads paddles warily across a marsh.

ASIDE FROM ITS STRIKING APPEARANCE, one of the redhead's most interesting characteristics is its courtship behaviour. Arriving back on the prairies in the spring, the males tingle with energy and excitement—splashing, displaying plumage, and making short flights about the marsh. Often several males compete simultaneously for the favours of the drab-coloured female. A variety of antics follows. The drakes pump their heads up and down, erect crests, frequently throw their heads back to touch their tails and chase each other about in fierce rushes. These manoeuvres are interspersed with the redhead's drawn-out siren call. Once paired off, the drake pursues its mate with zeal.

A northern shoveler drake displays its wings.

ONE OF THE MOST ABUNDANT DUCKS of the central prairies is the northern shoveler. Its long spatula-shaped bill is specially adapted for feeding on the microscopic life of the marsh. Tiny diatoms, ostracods and copepods can be strained from the mud and water by comblike structures of the bill called lamellae. However, most of the shoveler's diet is derived from larger plants and animals, especially freshwater snails and crustaceans, insects, and a variety of aquatic plant seeds. Frequently feeding cooperatively, shovelers swim in circles, foraging on aquatic organisms that have been stirred from the rich bottom sediment by other members of the flock.

FIVE SPECIES OF GREBES inhabit the prairie wetlands. Ranging in size from the large swan-like western grebe (length 45 cm/18 in.) to the dingy, pint-sized pied-billed grebe (length 23 cm/9 in.), the grebe family nevertheless shares many common characteristics. Aptly suited to an aquatic existence, all grebes have short, powerful legs and lobed toes to propel them swiftly underwater. All activities— feeding, sleeping, courting and even the entire reproductive process—take place on the water.

In the spring their courtship ceremonies are elaborate, each species acting out a distinctive and ritualized repertoire of swimming and diving maneuvres. Although grebes are usually quiet, the nesting marsh resounds with an assortment of brays, trills, chuckles, wails and whinnies. The nest is a soggy, floating structure anchored in a clump of emergent vegetation. When hatched, the chicks are ferried about the marsh on the backs of the parents until they are better able to fend for themselves.

Awkward when out of the water, eared grebes mate atop the floating nest.

FOLLOWING PAGES: A western grebe stretches a leg, displaying its specialized, lobed toes.

A red-necked grebe incubates its eggs in the seclusion of a bulrush clump.

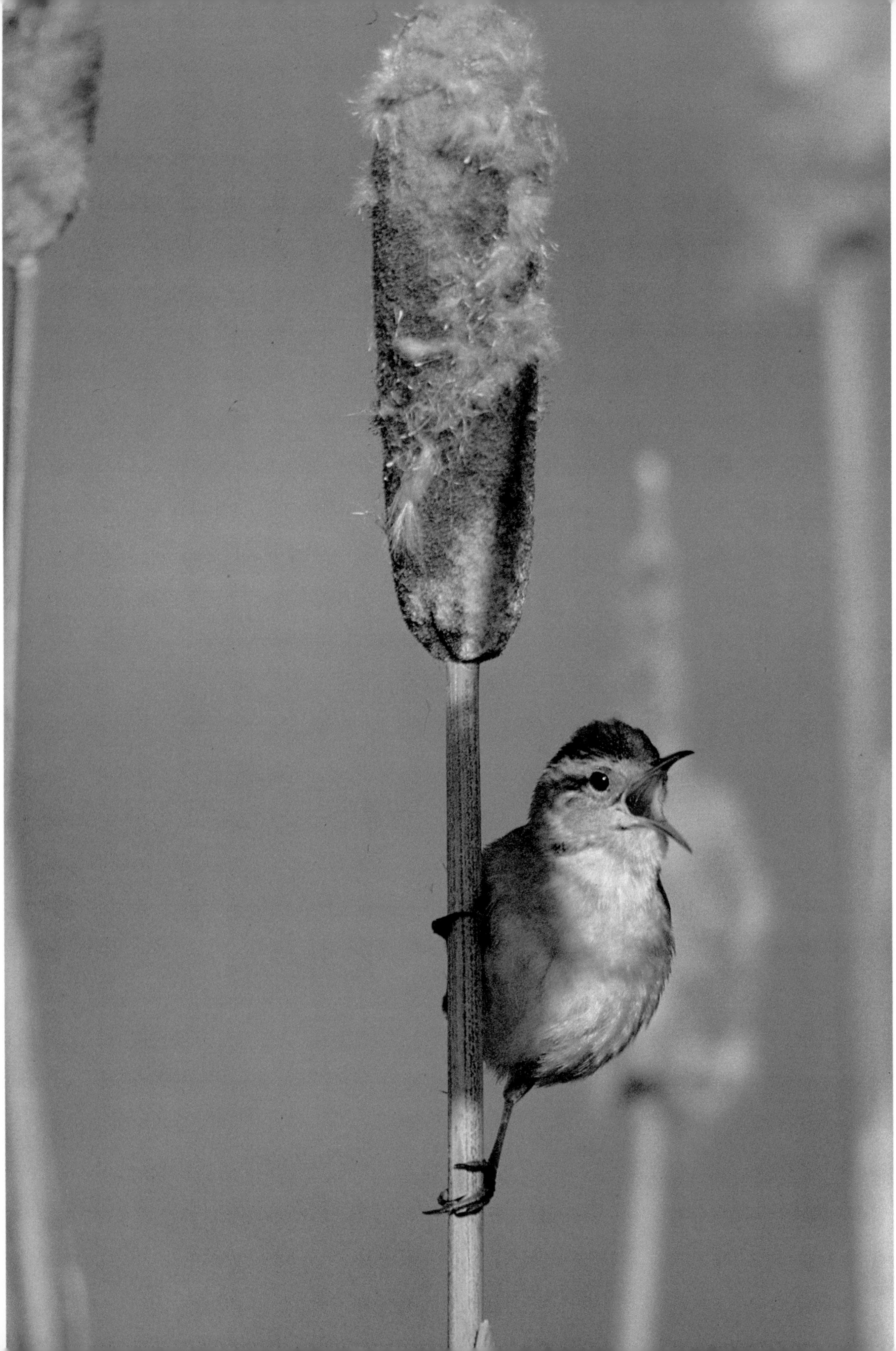

The cacophonous territorial call of the yellow-headed blackbird is accompanied by a display of wings and feathers.

THE MOST CONSPICUOUS BIRD on a prairie marsh in the spring is the yellow-headed blackbird. Perched atop a swaying cattail, the bright yellow helmet of the male is striking enough, but words can scarcely describe the bird's song: a grating combination of gurgles and clucks ending off with a drawn-out buzzing squeal. Throughout the spring the males energetically protect their individual breeding territories, chasing one another about the marsh. Meanwhile the more subdued female weaves a deep, basketlike nest of dead grasses, reeds or cattails among the upright stems of cattails or bulrushes. Her young leave the nest before they are two weeks old, remaining hidden in the close vegetation. Here they receive food from the parents until they are able to fly about a week later. By summer's end the yellowheads leave the marsh, often joining with red-winged blackbirds to form large flocks. Together they visit stubble fields, feeding on waste grains, weed seeds, grasshoppers and worms.

A long-billed marsh wren adds its peppy song to the wetland chorus.

The small Franklin's gull is the most strikingly patterned and graceful of the prairie gulls.

A Wilson's phalarope stretches a leg.

THREE SPECIES OF GULLS commonly breed on the central prairies: the Franklin's, California, and ring-billed. All are extremely beneficial to agriculture. When fields are being ploughed the gulls trail behind the farmer, plucking up the crickets, grasshoppers, cutworms, grubs and mice that are disturbed by the furrow.

All of these gulls reproduce in colonies. The Franklin's weaves a floating nest of reeds in shallow water, while the California and the ring-billed (the two white-headed species) build ground nests on islands that are safe from coyotes, skunks and foxes. When there are nestlings to feed, the gulls prey on the eggs and young of shorebirds, ducks, cormorants, and terns. At other times they scavenge dead fish and animals along the shore. The Franklin's gull catches gnats, mayflies, damselflies, and other insects which swarm above the water.

Surrounded by agricultural land, a slough becomes a haven for wildlife.

The marbled godwit is a large (length 41 cm/16 in.), wading bird of western sloughs, potholes and lakes.

An American avocet cautiously approaches its nest.

OF THE MANY SHOREBIRD SPECIES that frequent the prairie wetlands, the American avocet is considered to be the most beautiful. A slender, long-legged wader with a delicate up-curved bill, the avocet forages on the margins of shallow lakes and sloughs. The distinctive bill is used to stir up food from the muddy bottom and, partly opened, is swept through the water to catch small aquatic insects, crustaceans, seeds and other plant matter. Sometimes avocets feed in sizable flocks, as many as 300 parading *en masse* through the shallows.

The nest is a slight hollow on the shore of a wetland, usually lined with a few bits of dried grass. The olive-coloured, spotted eggs, tended by both adults, have a long incubation period—nearly three and a half weeks. However, the extra time inside the shell is well spent. On hatching the young are strong, lively and fully covered with down. A few hours later they are in the water swimming.

Riverlands

A solitary hunter, the lynx may be found in forested valleys of the northern prairies.

FOLLOWING PAGES: A prairie falcon springs off a rock face near its eyrie.

The smallest North American falcon, the American kestrel is a common nesting bird of the riverlands.

THE PRAIRIE FALCON is one of the swiftest birds of prey. With a streamlined torso, bullet-like head, short thick neck, powerful shoulders, and long pointed wings it is well suited for the dashing aerial manoeuvres that characterize its hunting behaviour. Much of the diet consists of birds, some of which are overtaken in direct low-level flight. Small birds—such as the prairie falcon's favourite target, the horned lark—are simply plucked out of the air. The falcon captures many others by diving swiftly from above, knocking them to the ground with a blow from its large talons.

During the spring the prairie falcon remains in the vicinity of the breeding habitat—badlands, coulees, rocky outcrops, canyons, or other steep, rocky sites. No nest is built; rather the falcon scrapes out a depression in the shallow soil or the loose gravel of a decomposing rock ledge. The spread of agriculture and the use of pesticides have caused a serious decline in population. The prairie falcon is classified as a threatened species by the US Department of the Interior.

Down-covered prairie falcons crowd around their mother at feeding time.

In the autumn, the quivering leaves of the aspen turn brilliant gold and yellow.

THE TREMBLING ASPEN is found over much of the western plains. The name is derived from its fine-toothed, long-stemmed leaves, which rustle in the slightest breeze. The trunk is smooth, creamy white, and marked by black warty patches. Although the aspen produces an abundance of buoyant, wind-carried seeds, the many groves found in the prairies are mainly propagated from the spreading root system. From root suckers the aspen is able to send up new trees and under ideal conditions whole forests develop in this manner.

In many ways stands of aspen enrich the wildlife communities of the plains. The protection they provide from the wind and sun allows many shrubs to flourish in the understory—principally wild rose, snowberry, chokecherry, hazelnut, and serviceberry. A variety of wild flowers also find niches in this community. Amidst the open sea of grass, aspen groves offer refuge to larger mammals. The bark is eaten by rabbits, mice and beaver. Deer browse the foliage, buds and twigs. Many birds that feed on the prairie nest in the trees and undergrowth.

A native of Europe, the attractive ox-eye daisy has spread across the prairies.

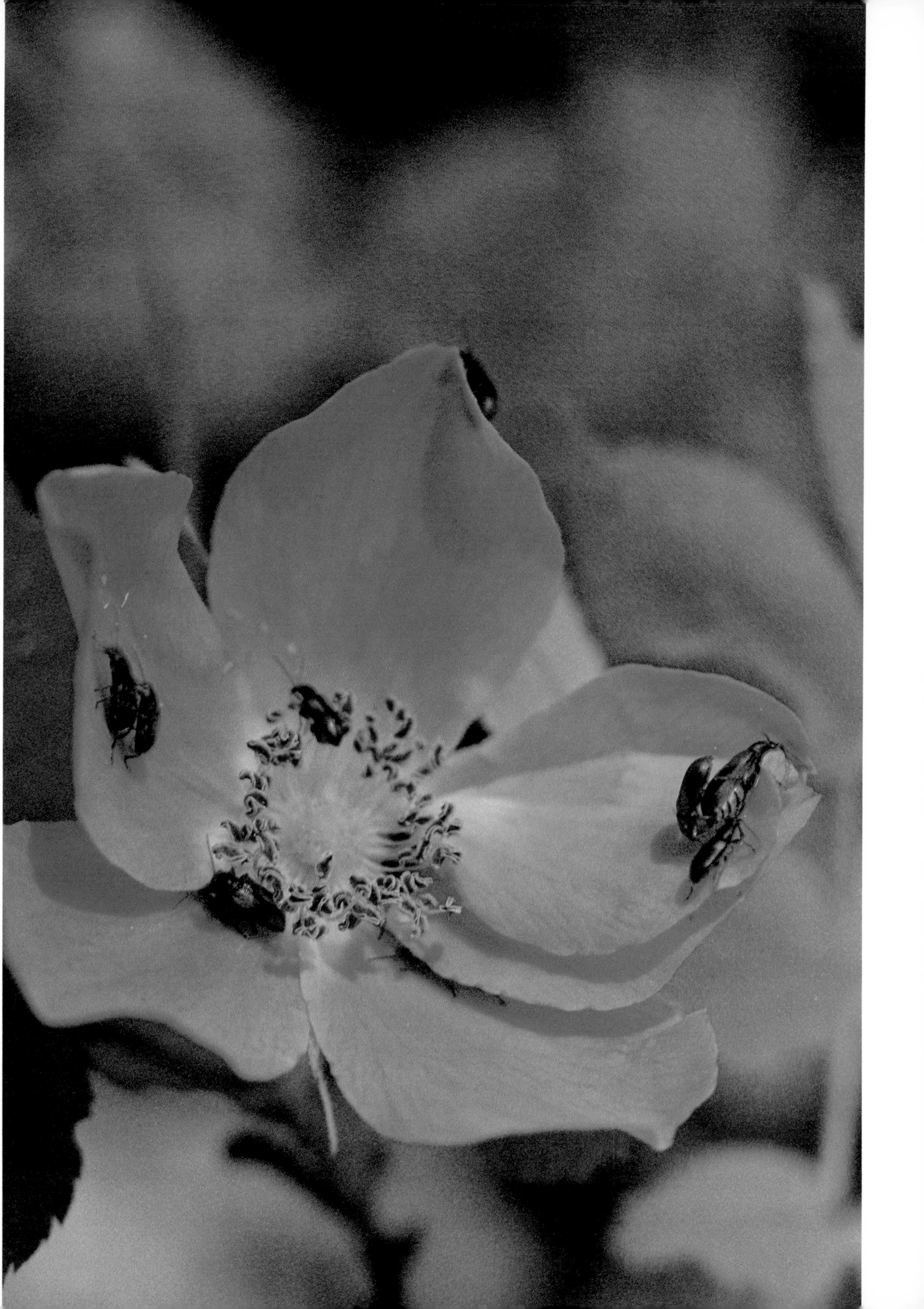

The vivid colour of a wild rose hip brightens the autumn landscape.

ONE OF THE BEST-KNOWN and most attractive shrubs of the western plains is the wild rose. Found in many varieties, it grows to about waist height in patches of prairie scrub, on the edges of bluffs, in coulees, and along roadsides and riverbanks. Through the late spring and summer the large, fragrant blooms enliven the landscape. The open-faced flowers usually have pink petals surrounding a shower of yellow gold stamens. The petals—supported by a green, ball-like struture called a calyx—eventually wilt and fall away. The calyx then turns red and takes on the more familir appearance of the rose hip. These fleshy fruits are filled with hairy seeds that have considerable food value for wildlife. The stems of the wild rose are armed with stiff prickles, making rose thickets a safe retreat for smaller animals (sharp-tailed grouse, pheasants, chipmunks, rabbits, and hares) fleeing from predators.

Beetles congregate on the petals of a wild rose.

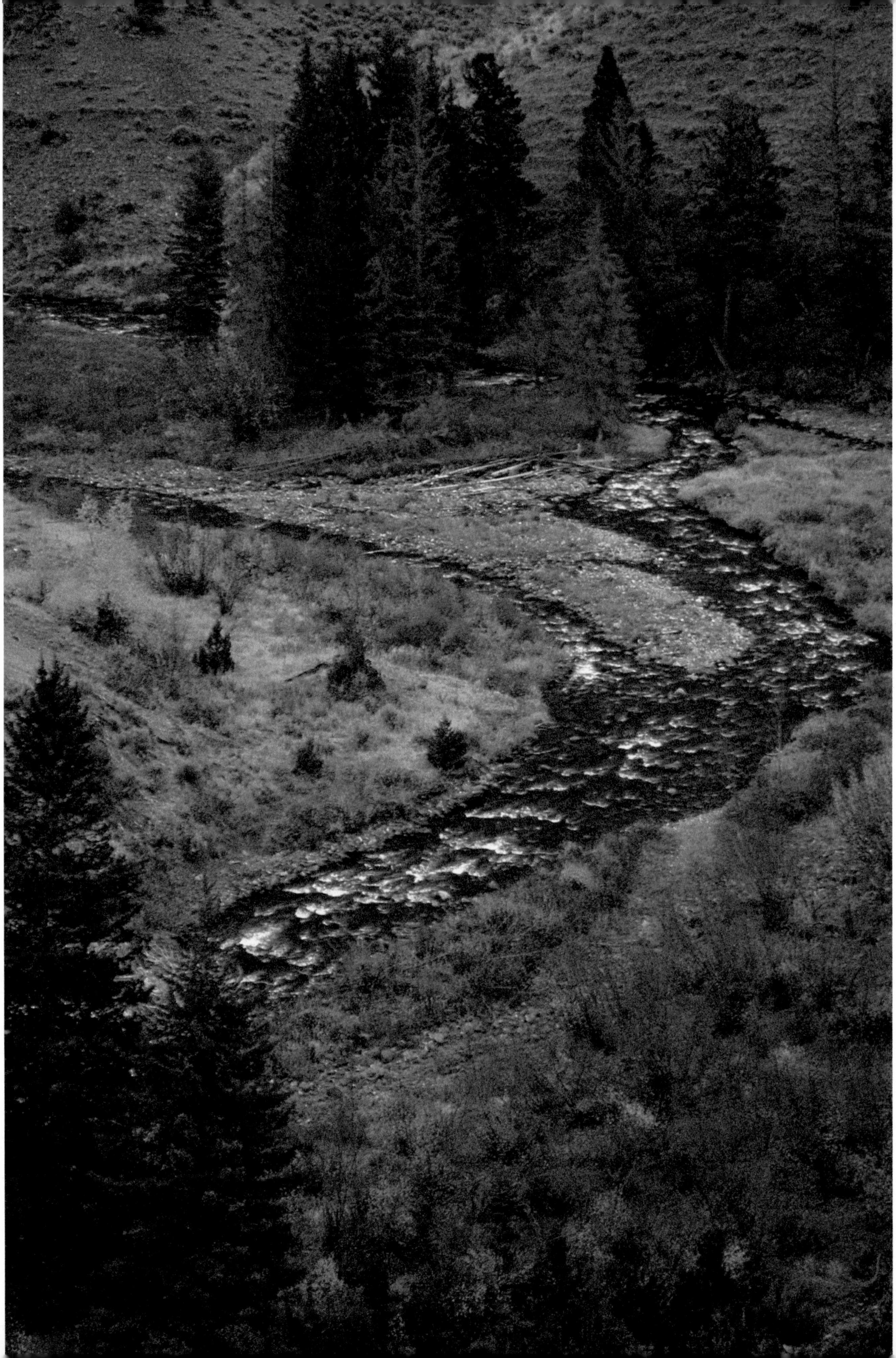

THE BLACK-BILLED MAGPIE'S scavenging tendencies make it one of the most familiar of prairie birds. Wherever an animal has been killed on the highway, a few magpies are likely to be seen pecking at the carcass. With each passing car they flutter up to a nearby fence post. Their flashy white wing patches, wedge-shaped streamer-like tails, and nasal 'yak-yak' calls make them a distinctive bird in any habitat. Their natural haunts are along the thicketed water-courses and among scattered trees of open country. Here they spend much of their time walking or hopping about on the ground, eating insects and grubs. Occasionally they will forage for ticks on the back of a mule deer or buffalo.

For its size (51 cm/20 in. long) the magpie builds a huge nest. Bulky domed-over structures of coarse sticks, some may be more than 1.2 m/4 ft high. However, the nests are quite functional and of benefit not only to magpies but to other birds as well. Owls, kestrels and hawks lay their eggs in abandoned nests, and robins and bluebirds seek refuge in them during storms.

A river valley in the short grass prairie provides shelter and breeding habitat for wildlife.

Standing on a mat of frozen algae, black-billed magpies feed at a duck carcass.

A common redpoll fluffs its feathers, trapping more air and improving its insulation against the cold.

LIKE MANY BIRDS that winter on the Prairies, common redpolls are especially suited to survive the cold. For their size (length 15 cm/6 in.) they have relatively more feathers than most other birds. To conserve heat, most of their muscle is concentrated about the body's core, there being no fleshy projections of legs, ears or tails outside the plumage. A special food-storage pouch is located in the esophagus to provide heat energy for the 14 to 15 hours of darkness each day during which the redpolls are unable to feed. Dangling from weeds or grasses projecting above the snow, they fill these crops with seeds selected for their high calorie content. Birch trees provide the most sought-after food, and the tiny birds cling to their drooping cones, removing seeds while the cast-off scales accumulate on the snow below. At nightfall they huddle together within the dense boughs of a conifer or take refuge in woodpecker holes. With the onset of spring they leave the Prairies for their nesting grounds in the forests of the north.

Cavities in these large balsam poplars may harbour squirrels, small owls and other birds during bitter prairie winters.

Trembling aspen, balsam poplar, white spruce and varied shrubs, grasses, sedges and aquatic plants line a stream on the northern prairie.

THE LAKES, MARSHES AND SLOW-FLOWING STREAMS of the West are the beaver's preferred habitats. Although a variety of trees and aquatic plants are eaten, the tender inner bark of trembling aspen is probably its favourite food. An active beaver topples an estimated 216 trees in a single year. Once the tree is on the ground, the beaver trims off the branches and drags them to the pond (sometimes a distance of 137 m/150 yds), where this big rodent does all its feeding. In the fall a store of branches is piled into deep water near the entrance to the lodge to provide a handy food source beneath the ice throughout the winter.

The beaver's practice of dam building is remarkable. The dams, which average 46 m/50 yds in length, are intended to flood the surrounding land to give the beaver easy swimming access to its food supply. Once completed, the massive, interwoven, mud-plastered structure is 3 m/9.8 ft wide at the base and over 2 m/6.6 ft high. It creates a pond deep enough to ensure that winter ice will not extend to the bottom and lock up the beaver's underwater larder.

MOOSE ARE FOUND PRIMARILY in the interior mountain region, where they inhabit thickets, alder swamps, lakeshores and aspen-birch parkland. Their range fingers out into the prairies along the forested river valleys that course down from the mountains and foothills. With knobby, stilt legs, humped shoulders, a long homely head and a droopy snout, the moose lays no claim to beauty. But it is the largest member of the deer family; the bulls stand almost 1.8 m/6 ft at the shoulder and sport magnificent shovel-shaped antlers that may be as wide as the moose is tall.

As a rule, moose are timid creatures and do not make unprovoked attacks on man. A cow will defend her calf by charging intruders, but she is more likely to withdraw. During the autumn rut the bulls can be dangerous and may charge if approached too closely. Moose are most likely to die of starvation, disease, and attacks by wolves or humans.

FOLLOWING PAGES: During a springtime snow flurry, a moose strikes a comic pose.

A beaver gnaws the tender bark of red-osier dogwood.

120

The ruffed grouse lives in brushy, wooded habitats and is preyed on by owls and large hawks.

On a limb near its nest a young great-horned owl clacks its beak threateningly.

FOLLOWING PAGES:
With a ground-squirrel in its talons, a ferruginous hawk alights at the nest.

THE WESTERN PLAINS are the stronghold of the ferruginous hawk. Although once common, its numbers have diminished owing to poison campaigns against their chief food source, the ground-squirrel. Dead, contaminated rodents are carried back to the nest for the young. Vandals also take a toll, shooting hawks as they perch and feed along roadsides. The silent remains of numerous bulky nests are still found on outcrops of rocky coulees and the cutbacks of many prairie rivers, attesting to the former abundance of this hawk. Composed of sticks, old bones, dried grass and cow dung, the nest is added to each year, in some cases attaining a height of 3 – 4 m/ 10 – 13 ft. Owing to the easy accessibility of many nests to ground predators, the ferruginous hawk is an aggressive defender of its territory, driving away foxes, owls, and even coyotes that venture near. In years when rodents are plentiful, more eggs are laid than normal, allowing populations to regain numbers lost in lean years. Besides ground-squirrels, ferruginous hawks eat grasshoppers, crickets, and birds.

A least chipmunk scampers along a rock outcrop.

THE LEAST CHIPMUNK is one of the many similar chipmunk species of the West. It prefers areas of tangled brush, logs and rocks, occupying coulees of the arid plains, stream valleys and forest openings. The least chipmunk appears above ground shortly after sunrise and spends the daylight hours in search of a variety of foods, zipping about the home territory to chase down a beetle, gather seeds, or feast on its favourite food—berries. As it forages, the chipmunk stuffs a considerable amount of material into its elastic cheek pouches, eventually carting the booty back to the burrow to be eaten in safety or stored for later use. Once winter sets in, the chipmunk is seldom seen above ground. It spends most of its time in deep sleep, waking only occasionally to grab a quick snack from one of its subterranean caches. As a small herbivore, the chipmunk is an important prey species for foxes, bobcats, weasels, hawks, owls and snakes.

Although seldom seen, the bobcat is one of the more common large predators of the plains.

THE BALSAM POPLAR is one of the few large trees found on the plains. Mature specimens occasionally attain heights of 30 m/98 ft and trunk diameters exceeding 1.2 m/4 ft. Flourishing in low-lying areas with rich soils, they provide nesting habitat for flickers, kestrels, owls, hawks, and other birds. The saplings often grow in pure stands. Their tender buds and twigs are browsed by deer and moose while beaver feed on the bark. Flowering before the leaves appear, the balsam poplar later discharges many fluffy, cotton-like, airborne seeds.

GROWING ALONG STREAMSIDES, shaded ravines and bottomlands, the red-osier dogwood is common throughout the prairie region. The most familiar feature of this straggling shrub is the bright red colour of its stems and branches, which are especially conspicuous during the winter. Often forming impenetrable thickets, the red-osier dogwood provides effective cover for wildlife, and its juicy, whitish berries are relished by rodents and birds.

A budding flower cluster of red-osier dogwood is surrounded by developing leaves.

In the early spring before emergence of the leaves, tiny clustered flowers in the form of drooping catkins appear on a stand of balsam poplar.

A raccoon relaxes in the crotch of a pine tree.

RACCOONS GENERALLY INHABIT FORESTED VALLEYS, preferring to be near water where much of their hunting is done. They also live in isolated stands of trees on the grasslands. An excellent climber, the raccoon spends most of its day snoozing in the crotch of a tree, although hollow logs and fox or marmot burrows may also be used. After sundown raccoons may venture out onto the prairie to feed on grasshoppers, crickets, frogs, mice, and voles. Fruit is also an important part of their diet and, using nimble forepaws, they pluck service berries, strawberries and currants. Crayfish are one of their favourite foods and these are carefully pulled from beneath rocks of streams and lakeshores.

During periods of extreme cold, raccoons remain inactive in their dens. Mating occurs during the winter and in a little over two months the young are born, usually three or four to a litter. An excellent mother, the female remains with her offspring, teaching them to hunt and climb, until the next mating season.

Red-osier dogwood brightens the late winter landscape.

Ever watchful, a cougar crouches atop a rotting deadfall.

AT ONE TIME COUGARS ranged over all the United States and southern Canada. Unfortunately their activities were incompatible with agriculture, and today they are found in fair numbers only in the wilderness mountain areas of the West. For the present, a few of these big cats survive in the river valleys and forested hillsides of the prairie states and provinces.

Cougars are the epitome of feline grace and power. Large males weigh up to 120 kgm/264 lbs. and measure 2.4 m/8 ft long (including the tail). Stealth and patience characterize their method of hunting. The cougar's eagerness as it inches forward is almost imperceptible, betrayed only by its gleaming eyes and the twitching tip of its tail. Once within range it makes an explosive dash toward the surprised quarry, pulls it down, and makes the kill quickly. Deer are the usual prey, although smaller animals are also eaten. Domestic livestock comprise an estimated four per cent of the diet. The cougar's lair is usually in a cave or rock crevice. Here the tiny kittens (400 gm/0.9 lb.) are born. They develop slowly and stay with the mother for a full year, feeding from her kills as they gradually learn to hunt for themselves.

A river rushes through a steep walled canyon.

BLACKBEARS are found in wooded river valleys of the plains. Here they wander the forests, eating a great variety of plants and animals. When first aroused from hibernation, they will eat spruce needles, birds and sprouting grass; and tear apart logs to get at the ants, ant eggs, grubs, and beetles within. During the summer, ripening raspberries, strawberries, serviceberries, cherries, currants, and crab apples are taken. More than three quarters of the diet consists of plant matter, with the remainder being made up mostly of insects and carrion.

A blackbear glares from the underbrush.

By hibernation time in late autumn the bears have grown fat and lethargic (a large male may weigh over 250 kgm/550 lbs). They crawl into a cave or hollow log, or curl up in the shelter of a deadfall to sleep through the winter. A secluded den becomes completely buried by snow, showing only a small breathing hole. Blind, naked, and puny, the cubs are born while the mother is dormant. They suckle for about eight weeks, emerging with the sow in April, rambunctious and fully furred.

An aspen bluff bordering a wooded river valley is flooded by morning sunshine.

A prairie rattlesnake lies coiled on the bank of a dry ravine.

THE MOST NOTORIOUS OF WESTERN REPTILES, prairie rattlesnakes are typical members of the pit viper family. On each side of the head, between the eye and nostril, is a heat-sensitive depression (the pit) that permits the rattler to locate warm-blooded animals in complete darkness at a distance of 0.5 m/20 in. Inside the broad head is a pair of curved hollow fangs. Usually folded back along the jaw, they swing forward instantaneously as the rattler opens its mouth to strike. The venom acts primarily on a victim's red blood cells, destroying them and causing the breakdown of tissue. The snake's activity is governed by temperature. In the spring and fall it hunts during the day, taking gophers, small ground squirrels and lizards. Hot summer weather forces the snakes to feed after dark. At this time their prey is more likely to be kangaroo rats, mice, and other nocturnal rodents.

A prairie dog town or ground-squirrel colony, a dry coulee, or rock outcrop of the badlands are all likely haunts of the prairie rattler. On the northern plains large numbers of these snakes may overwinter in a common denning site.

A stream meanders through dry, sage brush country.

The Canadian Toad spends the night hunting insects.

THE CANADIAN TOAD is a large (5 – 8 cm/2 – 3¼ in.) nocturnal species that is easily recognized by a bony hump between the eyes. In the spring its soft low-pitched trill emanates from the shallows of lakes and ponds throughout the northern grassland region. An adept excavator, it has horny tubercles on the hind feet to dig the burrow used as a refuge during the heat of the day.

Toads have never been thought elegant, but they do have a rough-hewn beauty all their own. Plopping along under shrubs and through grasses, the warted hunchback sifts mosquitoes, flies, beetles and other insects from the air and surrounding foliage by the thousands. After a short, careful stalk the toad flips out its sticky tongue, snagging its prey at distances up to 5 cm/2 in. Toads must be on the alert for a number of enemies, especially snakes. If attacked they are capable of secreting a toxic fluid from glands located on each side of the neck that inflames the mouth and throat of the predator.

Active both day and night, the common garter snake is found throughout the plains.

During the winter, evening grosbeaks feed on the winged seeds of green ash.

A MEMBER OF THE FINCH FAMILY, the evening grosbeak is about the size of a starling. It has a thick, cone-shaped bill adapted for cracking seeds. The striking plumage of the male is predominantly burnished gold, accentuated by black wings with large white patches that are especially evident in flight.

Most evening grosbeaks pass the spring and summer breeding season in a coniferous mountain habitat or in forests north of the Prairies. In the early winter many flocks migrate to the prairies, living along wooded river valleys and feeding on the seeds of chokecherries, pin cherries and serviceberries. Here they also find one of their favourite foods—the winged fruit of green ash and box elder. Their massive bills clip off the wings and crush the tough hulls, while the tongue fishes out the tender nut within. Grosbeaks move about the winter territory in loose flocks, twittering and chirping continuously throughout the day. In the early spring they harvest the emerging buds of poplars and willows before dispersing to the breeding territories.

A grove of green ash with an understory of chokecherry.

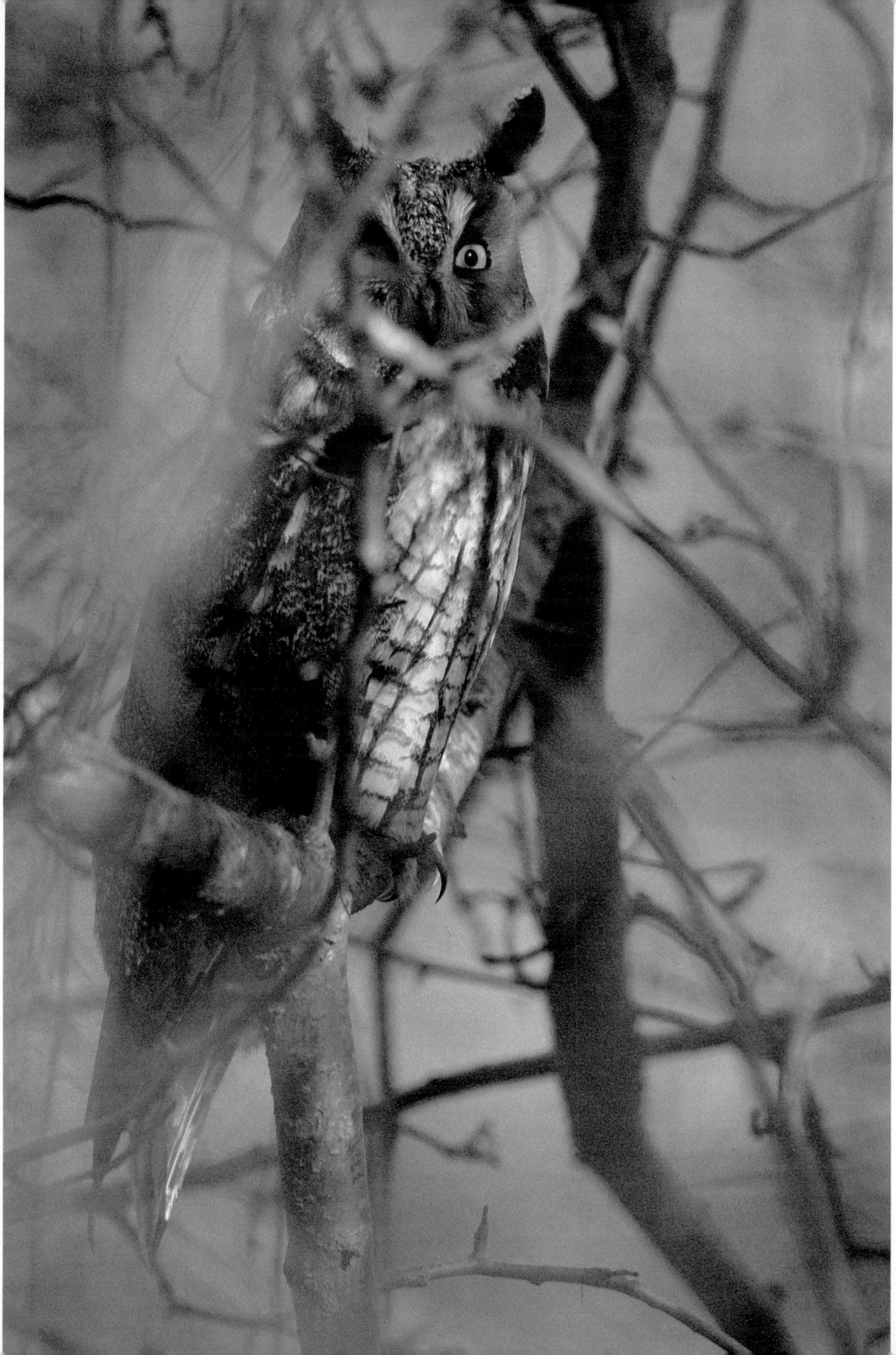

An hour or two before dawn is the favoured hunting time of many owls.

THE LONG-EARED OWL is one of the most secretive birds of prey. By day it roosts in dense stands of aspens, tangled bottomland thickets or wooded coulees. If alarmed it stretches out its angular frame, compresses its earthy, bark-toned feathers, and raises the head tufts to take on the prosaic appearance of a snag or branch. Almost exclusively a night-time hunter, the long-eared owl kills mice, shrews and occasionally songbirds. Its keen eyes are almost as big as a human's. But even more remarkable are the ears: long, asymmetrical slits hidden behind the facial discs, they can pinpoint and lead to the capturing of a live mouse in complete darkness. Flight feathers are equipped with mufflers in the form of comb-like projections and fringes that eliminate the sound of attack.

Long-eared owls usually lay their eggs in the abandoned nests of other birds such as magpies, herons and crows. Often the nests are only 2 – 3 m/6 – 10 ft above the ground. The young hatch out several days apart, and usually the smallest owlets do not survive, often owing to attacks by their larger brothers and sisters.

A long-eared owl tries to remain inconspicuous in its daytime roost.

Index of Plates

Selected References

Banfield, A.W.F. *The Mammals of Canada.* Toronto and Buffalo: University of Toronto Press, 1974.

Behler, John L. and King, F. Wayne. *The Audubon Society Field Guide to North American Reptiles and Amphibians.* New York: Alfred A. Knopf, 1979.

Braithwaite, Max. *The Western Plains.* Toronto: N.S.L. Natural Science of Canada Ltd., 1970.

Budd, A.C. *Budd's Flora of the Canadian Prairie Provinces.* Ottawa: Research Branch, Agriculture Canada, 1979.

Burt, William H. and Grossenheider, Richard P. *A Field Guide to the Mammals.* Boston: Houghton Mifflin Company, 1976.

Cormack, R.G.H. *Wild Flowers of Alberta.* Edmonton: Hurtig Publishers, 1977.

Costello, David F. *The Prairie World.* New York: Thomas Y. Crowell Company, 1969.

Farb, Peter. *Face of North America.* New York: Harper & Row, 1963.

Godfrey, W. Earl. *The Birds of Canada.* Ottawa: National Museum of Canada, 1966.

Hamilton, W.J. *American Mammals.* New York: McGraw-Hill, 1939.

Hardy, W.G. (editor). *Alberta, a Natural History.* Edmonton: Hurtig Publishers, 1967.

Hosie, R.C. *Native Trees of Canada.* Don Mills, Ontario: Fitzhenry and Whiteside, 1979.

Klots, Elsie B. *The New Field Book of Freshwater Life.* New York: G.P. Putnam's Sons, 1966.

Milne, Lorus and Margery. *The Audubon Society Field Guide to North American Insects and Spiders.* New York: Alfred A. Knopf, 1980.

Nelson, J.G. and Chambers, M.J. (editors). *Vegetation, Soils and Wildlife.* Toronto: Methuen Publications, 1969.

Peattie, Donald Culross. *A Natural History of Western Trees.* Boston: Houghton Mifflin, 1953.

Salt, W. Ray and Salt, Jim R. *The Birds of Alberta.* Edmonton: Hurtig Publishers, 1976.

Shelford, Victor E. *The Ecology of North America.* Chicago: University of Illinois Press, 1974.

Terres, John K. *The Audubon Society Encyclopaedia of North American Birds.* New York: Alfred A. Knopf, 1980.

Vance, F.R., Jowsey, J.R. and Mclean, J.S. *Wildflowers Across the Prairies.* Saskatoon: Western Producer Prairie Books, 1977.

Weaver, J.E. and Albertson, F.W. *Grasslands of the Great Plains: Their Nature and Use.* Lincoln, Nebraska: Johnson Publishing Company, 1956.